American Dreams

Joni Järvi-Laturi

Kustantaja: BoD, Books on Demand, Helsinki, Suomi.
Valmistaja: BoD, Books on Demand, Norderstedt, Saksa.
ISBN: 978-952-80-6062-8

Contents

Some Miscellaneous Notes Concerning a Film Screenplay About America

joku suojelee jotakuta
se on kristityn rakkaus, kristityn rakkaus,
maskuliinisuus,

salaiset agentit
supervoimat yhdellä nuorella, naiivilla miehellä
äidin hoivavietti

The artist (writer) saves a man from drowning. The man is eternally grateful for the artist and befriends him.

When I watch presentations of America's kind and peaceful states and the cities within them, I cry. Is there a greater proof of American Providence?

The superpower is a glimpse at the future from the man's body language.

To live and love within some peaceful community filled with kind, decent, intelligent, talented and wise people. To live in the kingdom of heaven and to feel nothing but love and do nothing but good.

America, she was made to be loved and not analyzed.

These tears are strong, filled with sorrows and joys of past loves and of future passions.

Oswald Image – window to soul, window to an imperfect, weak lover as well.

Love grows silently, wisely like an eagle flying alone.

The strong, silent man.

Hollywoodian corner.

The American Dreamer.

Sentimental cinema.

Coin.

Gift to America, after death. A bracelet

Loner.

THE INTRODUCTION

Dark tent. Light. Book.

NARRATOR
Here stranded from almost every place on Earth sat a reader
of the purest wonder ever imagined, a quiet breath, a succulent literature,
a muscular tradition, except that this was not at all the same language agreed upon, a
language that revolved around divine secrets and delicacies.

A godliness of a reader's island,
a heaven of a lonely reader's literal palace,
an American corner, a Hollywood corner
of greatness and individualism and moral virtues.

No wonder the reader, the dignified reader, was a minority in everything, and
everywhere he went.

Greatness as a crime, individualism as a sin, were a nightmarish surrounding to live
in but paradoxically they were also the blessing of his life.

Because the island had its protectors,
the reader felt excitement and love
from the great commentators and defenders of
the greatest system ever built – The U.S. of America,
but they existed only in his mind.

He feared that the sophistication would end,
that Western civilization would end.
There was no greatness left, no magnificence
to protect and the world had progressed too rapidly to the new era,
without knowing what to stand for and what to fight for.

Forest. Light. Book.

NARRATOR
The forest was dark and dreary,
with two kinds of creatures,

the wicked and the profane. The snakes
represented the wickedness of nature
and the man represented the saintliness of dignity.

Night. Light. Book.

NARRATOR
The night had been violent for centuries.
The man had been in love with America,
and secretly loving conservative Republicans,
in his home country of Finland.

The City. Light. Book.

NARRATOR
The man loved the great wise conservative commentators.
and effeminately liked their videos on the internet,
a small, effete, but also an important and nice modern gesture.

He started walking downtown, hating the dreary, drunken chaos that so many people
had succumbed to, reading a story about America on the bus. And here is how the
story went.

Finland and America

If a Finn has great feelings towards America and holds American values as paramount, as something greater than Finnish values, well that is comparable to witnessing UFO sightings on your own or seeing Bigfoot on your own. Nobody believes you. Nobody believes your feelings and emotions towards the greatest country on Earth. Americophilia tends to be lonely and feel lonely. The detractors usually point to America's multitudinous gun massacres and the great number of poor people and the societal ills such as expensive health care and student loan debt. These are valid points. Even though these same left-leaning Finns are hopelessly addicted to Facebook, an American invention as well as to YouTube, another American invention, they still hold America accountable for many ills.

If there is one lamentation I hold about my country of birth, Finland, it is the narrowness of our psyche and, sometimes, our way of life. There is something small and prosaic about our lack of dissent, the dissent of the spirit. We can be cynical people without a moralistic emphasis on social affairs. I sometimes think that Finns are copies of each other in some essential things. I crave for great moralistic, artistic and idealistic heroes, that my country, in its emphasis on welfare and equality, doesn't always give me. Not to mention the awful experiences of nihilistic youngsters in my youth and a certain, weird nihilistic ethos without a moralistic idealism I so much crave into my life. The lack of a moralistic approach to life, which Judeo-Christian conservative America offers, seems lonely while living in Finland. In point of actual fact, when one talks about good and evil and morality, one is shunned, sometimes even laughed at, in the wonderfully equal country of Finland.

Still, I love Finland as well. I have spent two amazing and memorable decades here, the 1990s and the 2010s, thanks to the communities that gave me so much fascinating and mind-blowing experiences where my hometown Tampere was at the centre of a communal comfort, where life was like spending time with two families, my own family and the city of Tampere. In 1990s my childhood was athletic, I played hockey and soccer and I estimate that I met a thousand lovely people through school, leisure and sports. In 2010s I spent years in a mental rehabilitation community and Tampere yet again felt like an enormous family. It was incredible.

But, deep down, I always sought for something more, and I always knew I was going to be a true artist. Early on, I felt as if I represented many of the forbidden dreams, feelings, thoughts and ideas contrary to the modern age. I always searched for more and what I searched for was everything that the modern world had tragically forgotten or lacked. Finland didn't listen to my voice, as a young, struggling artist, even though I heard from at least three or four different parts of colloquial discourse and hearsay that I was a genius.

I grew to despise the celebration of mediocrity, and the fact that it was much easier to declare one self a mediocrity than a genius. I also discovered many intellectual cowards who catered to the group, and not the individual.

I also despised the sameness of each thought, the sameness of each experience, the sameness of each subjective feeling. I felt that it destroys the uniqueness of certain thoughts, the uniqueness of certain experiences and the uniqueness of certain subjective feelings. I don't want to sacrifice my greatness over someone's great moment, however great the moment might be. True, individualistic, achievement-oriented greatness is not normal and is certainly not common and is certainly not as small as a mundane feeling or experience.

Man was created to be great and achieve great things and greatness stands for something, and it can be measured and detected. The willingness to be small, the offensive submission to small passions, to small ideas, to small moments, to small joys, to a small, like-minded group, as well as the relativistic subjectivity of each smallness being as important and relevant as greatness has always struck me as being a cowardly and an unbearably collectivistic notion.

I feel as if the emphasis on equality destroys greatness. Where have all the geniuses gone? Maybe they haven't? Nowadays, reality is seen as art. The equality of each thought, of each action, of each moment and of each intention seems outrageously vulgar and narrow-minded in a world where the gap between unique greatness and common mediocrity is so wide.

I also despised collectivism, the notion where the group is more important and unique than the individual. We are not always stronger together, we are sometimes weaker and worse together. America has always seemed like a haven of greatness, of big ideas, big people and big innovations. The fact that most of humanity's innovations and fresh ideas come from America, struck me as a good example of America's divine providence.

I also despised moral relativism. I had seen so much meanness, of evil words and outright collective nihilism, where nobody is happy and everyone is cruel, that I despise the subjective view of morality. In my view, one is either a decent person or one is not. This attribute, decency, depends on your each individual action that are derivative from your own moral value system. Meanness is a sin, it is not a harmless and a natural part of human condition, it is a personal choice which one has to be accounted for.

Small Note on America

I consider Americans as my dear friends. I feel a strange, incessant and curious sympathy to the greatest country of Earth, The United States and its people. I dream of living in a nine-million dollar mansion in Beverly Hills, I dream of visiting an American grocery store and purchasing items there (the exotic candy, the sparkling sodas, the joy-inducing cigarette packs and the nutritious cheese brands), I sometimes cry tears of joy when I watch presentations of American cities on YouTube, I love the history of Hollywood and the mystique of the lives of famous celebrities, I love the pop culture and its famous quotes and anecdotes. And I love the fact that the United States is the world police.

I have always been interested in alternative America, in psychedelic America, in hippie America. But I grew up to find the greatest solace in conservative America. I admired their arguments, I thirsted for their moralistic wisdom, I considered them big brothers and sisters to me and my philosophy of life. I felt that this part of me was not seen or heard in Finland and it was seen as strange or foreign, if not insulting to Finland's left-wing, secular hegemony.

I always thought how an American conservative commentator loved America. I was subconsciously obsessed with those light-hearted, humorous comic reliefs they referenced in their more serious political speak. Those "soft" and "pointless" moments that revealed what books, music and movies they loved, those were the moments I always hunted. I loved their references to classic literature, like to the pity-inducing Karamazov Brothers written by a conservative Russian Fyodor Dostoevsky or to the music of Johann Sebastian Bach which has brought even many secular people to tears.

The sympathetic affection for the common, simple people that conservatives so often hold with the passionate admiration for great artists like myself, always felt like an interesting combination. It felt like a divine combination, as well. I felt special and loved by someone.

My Conservative Sympathies

Here are some of my conservative sympathies. I love the philosophy concerning life in general and I notice that life and politics are different things. I find conservatism, especially in its greatest forms, an incredibly important and healthy philosophy.

Feminism.

Feminists tend to hate the patriarchal structures of Western societies and rebel against them. This is a common view of the left. I always wondered where is the patriarchy? Where is it? If one considers the fact that 99 percent of those feminist women who want to have mindless, emotionally cold casual sex with men, want the men to be strong because women in generally are very attracted to strong men, even stronger than them, sometimes. So where is the patriarchy they so hate and oppose? There is no patriarchy without strong men. Strong men have built cities, joined police forces and protected the weak.

If one considers the fact that in bars where young people drink alcohol and mess around and talk about fashionable things, men are almost always the loudest in the group, maybe even to the point of being offensive and barbaric and behaving like pigs and talking aggressively. And young women might love it, and they might love being dominated and quiet, with someone being more menacing than them, with strong men leading the conversation.

I also believe in a different West than the feminists. I believe we revel in freedom, there is very much freedom and very much equality in the West, but there is also inequality. Even those people who believe in equality are judgmental and rough towards some people they don't like, because it is the human condition and it is easily noticeable even in the most feministic, equality-believing people.

I don't consider myself an anti-feminist, but I do have anti-feminist sentiments. My anti-feminist sentiments are actually very matriarchal, instead of being patriarchal. I believe in the goodness of women, the warmth, the motherliness, the softness, the comfort, the gentle, empathetic strength, more than in the coldness, the toughness, the beastliness, the narcissism that some young feminist women are emulating. I wish to see a world where women are raised differently, so they don't start to copy men, or the classical male pathologies like sadism, roughness and control. I have noticed that many young women emulate male toughness and it just simply looks terrible.

Winners and losers.

The American value of "winners and losers" has affected me and gained my sympathy. The Finnish value of "everyone is equal" alienates me because it blindly forgets the difference between good and bad. There are differences between people. To not say so, undermines the intelligence of every person and doesn't notice the qualitative difference of people. Difference is unequal, in morals and in skills.

Dignity.

I am a church person more than a bar person.

The new millennium has seen a rise in vulgar, angry, narcissistic behaviour that the humanity has been exposed to, first by reality television, and secondly by Instagram and Facebook profiles, where every Westerner can post news about their lives. Facebook and Instagram are obsessions. They are addictions. I don't always like the lame jokes, the commercial narcissism, the elevation of the platitudinous and stupid over the serious and the great.

Nowadays people tend to celebrate stupidity. We used to have talents but nowadays we tend to copy the old. The past is constantly ahead of our time.

In Fawlty Towers, the main character Basil Fawlty is by today's standards a sexist, racist, bigoted, fascistic misogynistic loser but I always found this character to speak for the lonely and unpopular views of the hated, lonely, intelligent man. In one episode called The Psychiatrist, Basil hates the hotel's new customer, a young and popular man, who is thought of as sexy by Basil's wife, Sybil. The customer is wearing a shirt open and his chest is visible with golden medals hanging around his neck. Basil even asks his wife that "do we have enough bananas this week?" referring to the customer whom he sees as primitive and distastefully open. As Basil fights with Sybil about what is charming, being dignified or being more open, Sybil says:
   "Tell me Basil – what is it about the Mediterranean type that antagonizes you so? Is it because women find them attractive?"
B: "Sybil I…"
S: "You seem to think that we girls should be aroused by people like Gladstone and Earl Haig and Baden Powell. Don't you?"
Basil says: "Well at least they had a certain dignity. It's hard to imagine Earl Haig wandering around with his shirt open to the waist – covered with identity bracelets is it?"

I absolutely loved Basil's response and found it to be a warning to future generations about the lack of dignity and style. In my view, the relegation of dignity is a real problem. And many men feel this as well. I see many young people as behaving like narcissistic children, when I want them to behave like adults with dignity.

Abortion.

Hardly anybody can deny the vast innocence of children, the sweetness of their innocence that can touch us to tears. I have lately found little children to be comical also. And their comical trait is related to their innocence. It makes us laugh but it also makes us awe. So, that is why the innocence of a child has to be protected. I also think that a child having a mother and a father is very important. The child receives the example of both sexes, hopefully the strong and wise influence of the father and the equally strong and wise example of the mother. A child has to be taught reason and morality at an early age. I also believe that children should be spoiled but that is a separate issue from instilling values to the child.

Hardly any of us feels joy and relief when watching pictures of aborted children with their limbs cut off and their brain sucked out. The whole notion of death being celebrated, whether suicide, abortion, violence, makes me vomit. When people think the sexual freedom and the sexual choices a woman makes are more important than killing a baby, I find this position to be narcissistic. It is narcissistic, vapid and dangerous to position mistakes in one's sex life to be more important than killing a baby. I often wonder why do people celebrate abortion becoming legal with such joy? But at the same time they want the death penalty to be obliterated.

The Personality Traits Which Reveal My Love for America

At Pitkäniemi mental hospital I liked the company of caretakers and nurses a bit more than patients. I think the reason for this was the exciting wisdom and maturity of the people who ran the mental hospital.

I always had a tendency to trust my parents and do what they say. I resented any outsiders, meaning bureaucrats and social workers who came in between me and my family. They viewed that I was spoiled and also raised to be in a prison and raised to be dependent and weak.

But the irony is that those bureaucrats and social workers wanted to replace my parents, to become my new parents. I thought it was a sin to meddle in me and my family's life. I still do.

My parents were capitalists and they had a certain careful conservative outlook on life. They were quite secular meaning that they believed in evolution and not the Bible. They detested the ascetic criticism of consumerism because they thought that the market economy had to be supported because the system was right. I find materialism and consumerism to be joyful values, as joyful as being in touch with nature. I also find them to be soulful values. I love big cities, big buildings, big supermarkets and big everything. Without them, the world would stagnate. My parents found money to be an important and sacred thing in life and they were very cautious with it.

I always loved the classics, in anything. I love classic board games, classic card games, classic films, classic music, classic books, classic actors. I like class. I always felt comfort in classics since I was a little child. I lived the classic decade of the 90s (in 1995-1999) and they were the greatest years of my life. I always compare everything to the 1990s. It was such a social, beautiful and innocent life where I had no worries at all. My father drove me to hockey matches, I played soccer as well and I met many hundreds of people during this particular decade. Words cannot describe it but I think the old Scottish song Auld Lang Syne captures the nostalgia and the brotherhood of Messukylä, the school I went to.

Then the 1990s was dead. The decade of class and innocence was gone. And the 2000s arrived. In 2003 I had already become depressed and I was mentally ill, even though my family did not know it. Our family has mental illness in it. The destruction of such an innocent age and the replacement of it with something uglier was devastating. The world had changed through reality television and other low-brow phenomena to something weird. Also, 9/11, the Iraq war and the killing of Swedish minister Anna Lindh, the Dutch politician Pim Fortuyn and Theo van Gogh, another Dutchman, was particularly traumatic. Something had changed, violently. At least I thought so. I also was bullied verbally and I felt a tremendous alienation in school. I listened to the consoling songs of The Smiths and watched videos of American conservatives and liberals. I also felt that the commercialization of beautiful things led to a world where soul was forgotten. True artistic genius and strength arose from the grassroots. I felt that there would be no grassroots in the future and everything started to become commercial and shallow, like The American Idol, which in my view, destroyed music in some way.

This was probably the reason American conservatism started to appeal me.

My Strange Year of 2020

I have had four psychoses. In 2008, in 2014 and twice in 2020. My third psychosis in
the beginning of 2020 was due to a mysterious Scientologist who wrote me
sarcastically, claiming that I was a closeted homosexual. I had homoerotic thoughts
back then and I have always considered myself gay in spirit, but at the same time I
have considered people who think I am gay, to be wrong. The scientologist brought
my gay sides open to me. But nevertheless, I consider myself a heterosexual now and
at the same time still hold effeminate feelings and thoughts and dreams. In the army,
back in 2007, I was called J. Lo (as in Jennifer Lopez) with tough love. So, I have
always been considered to be a homosexual because I have my effeminate traits and
effeminate passions.

The year 2020 was weird. It was mystical and strange, unbelievable and amazing. I
went to a mental hospital twice that year. And the hospital was even more mystical
and strange. I think everyone knew each others' thoughts in that facility and I
received lot of love there. I admired the patients and the nurses because they were
very kind people.

But the thing why 2020 was so amazingly weird was that amazingly weird situations
happened. I gained superpowers because of my correspondence with the Scientologist
and my psychotic delusions were powerful. On the internet, I thought that everyone
had noticed me and noticed how amazing and marvellous I was. I felt like a God. In
the place where schizophrenia patients went for an injection, Tipotie, to be exact, the
patients called me a God. Something was happening. I think my body language was
sensitive and the patients talked in a way that noticed my body language. Either they
got some answers to their future problems from my body language or something else.
They also had watched my Facebook profile and watched my posts which were
mystical and powerful. They admired me and I love the love they gave me. They
treated me like a God. It was very nice. The love I felt was amazing.

On the internet I watched a Bernie Sanders rally and Sanders mentioned Shakespeare
and the crowd went wild. I thought every video had a message for me. The television
and YouTube, I felt that every video was speaking to me. The intellectual dark web, I
felt I was part of it, and ever since the Scientologist wrote to me, I thought that the
internet itself, my internet had changed.

I felt like a Jesus, I felt like conservatives needed my ideas and got some of their
ideas through me. I even had many ideas concerning world peace. I thought of a
sauna and an airplane, something about sauna and an airplane assuring world peace to

everywhere. I was wrong, the world didn't change to a more peaceful place. I also posted an image where there was the peace sign and the subtext "Trump 2020, an unusual hope." Later I realized that Trump had signed a peace deal in the Middle East and conservatives thought that he deserved a Nobel Peace Prize. I just sensed this for some reason. I also saw a dream where a young leftist political commentator Michael Brooks had finally gone to a place where he can wear a business suit, like a businessman. Couple of days later, Brooks had passed away, tragically.

I saw Michael Knowles and Dave Rubin as being my big brothers on the internet. They sent me signs, but later I thought it was just my own imagination. I also felt that the CIA had known my powers when I was a child and that they knew I was going to be an asset in the future.. While watching an episode of the first season of X Files, I thought that I was an UFO, or something like that. I relived the Tampere of 1990s in that series.

Also, in that year, I saw footage from 2016 or 2017, where Hillary Clinton said "snake" in a wicked and humorous manner and I felt that the snake was me, coming to revenge in the 2020 election, to Donald Trump, without me knowing it. I felt that my writing was snake-like.

I saw that a Finnish politician Jussi Halla-aho watched to left and center and right with his eyes in some old interviews. I thought this was a message for me. I had three Facebook profiles Divina Joni (which meant left-wing passions), Joni Järvi-Laturi (which meant my own passions, the center passions) and Kirjailija Joni Järvi-Laturi (which meant my right-wing passions). After this I saw many videos, one in Finland where Anna Kontula watched left, center and right with her eyes, as well as Michael Moore doing this and many videos of Finnish vlogger Sofia Keitaanranta doing this. Also, in the second stint in Pitkäniemi, a male nurse got to know me and he watched in three different sides while talking to me (which at first scared me a bit).

In the second mental hospital stint, at 2020, I saw my old acquaintance from Tipotie, as having political power. He used his cell phone and was boasting that he did some kind of detective work or something like that. I still don't know what he did, but it was amazing that a young mental patient had so much power, even international power.

I really miss the good parts of this incredibly weird year 2020. But I still thank God that the year 2021, is much more normal and more boring in a good way. I really don't miss my delusions. But it was an intriguing experience to feel like being a God and especially being a God, whom America needed.

My American Fantasies

I have to dream often for dreams are the fuel of my soul. I haven't dreamt before
what my life would be like in America. I consider this essay as my fantasies
concerning life in America.

First off, I would like to get acquainted with The Wine Country in California. I would
walk the fields of the vineyard of The Sonoma Mountain AVA while eyeing the
magnificent horizon where there are the Mayacamas Mountains. I would stay in a
hotel in Napa Valley and swim in the pool and enjoy sunbathing on the patio for two
weeks. I would enjoy the restaurants and eat shrimps and chicken while drinking
different sorts of cocktails and other creatively made alcohol drinks.

At night I would swim in the ocean with a friend. I have dreamt of different sorts of
friends. My one fantasy friend is someone like the late writer Hunter S. Thompson. If
this fantasy would materialize, I would have no shortage of fun. The intriguing detail
about Hunter was that he didn't give his friends an easy, smiling ride but that he
respected his friends even though he didn't show his affection that well because he
was shy in some sense. I have even thought of doing psychedelic drugs with this
friend, to mess around in a hotel room and going to a desert somewhere in California
to experience the effects of the psychedelic drugs. But in reality I would probably not
take drugs with anyone because I don't want to take the risk because I am
schizophrenic.

I have often thought of a road trip through America. This is a very popular dream
expressed in many comedy films like Dumb & Dumber, Road Trip and Plains, Trains
and Automobiles. Sitting on the car while it drives through America would be a
pleasure to the extreme, a comfortable joy where I would only have to sit and wonder
the night sky and the buildings and the streets with their shadows and their nightly
atmosphere.

I would drink every drink in some nice theme bar. I would watch fifteen movies in a
row in some film group. I would live in a nine-dollar mansion filled with nice rooms.
I would experience the desert at night while it would rain immensely and the water
would drop on my jacket and I would feel the rain as some kind of poetry.

I also have a more sympathetic dream. I dream of living in a town where there would
be a lot of conservatives and a lot of Christian believers. I hope the Christians and the

conservatives would like movies, books and music. The greatest feeling would be to watch Bergman's films and talk about them philosophically with a civilized priest.

I would also dream of playing hockey with some sporting group. Play music at night in some forgotten, densely populated area. Shoot weapons to different kinds of targets. And also, I would love to be in a nightclub and drive to a big, empty hall or a factory and experience the quiet beauty of that vast, magnificent building. And maybe to lie on top of the building and watch the night sky with some perfect, patient friend and talk philosophy, wondering about classic old and new films.

My Christian Sympathies

For much of the time, I have had admiring thoughts about Christianity but also deep sense of faith in God. I usually don't want to talk about my feelings and thoughts about Christ and Christianity. I have felt that I tip-toe on the issue of Christ and Christianity, flirt with Christianity but not completely encapsulating the idea of Christ and the belief in Christ. I consider myself almost a Christian which probably is a bit irritating to true believers of Christ.

I really don't like that the Greek gods, the gods before Christ, are considered better than the Christian God by many secularists. I also don't care for a completely anti-God, secular outlook on life. I think secularism makes people less deep and less decent. Everything seems to be permitted and there is no moral battle in life. Of course this is a generalization but generalizations are viewed as being mostly true. However I find the spirituality of many secularists to be very fruitful and sympathetic ways of dealing with the mysteries of life. The Christian God introduced the world a person who loved the whole human race and each individual human being and he suffered because of them. The Christian God also elevates the small, simple, ordinary people as divine, and they are celebrated even though they are not famous or rich. The worst plights and the most horrendous sufferings are met with an eternally loving God who forgives the sinner and heals the farthest people of his providence. The God that is loving and good and not a chaotic madman like many Greek Gods are with their dysfunctional relationships.

Christianity and Christ give me immense amounts of other comfort as well. I think it is a comforting, cute, charming and beautiful thing when a good man or a good woman believes in Christ. The most awe-inspiring thing is when the Christ-like Christians are also open-minded and free-thinking individuals open to many kinds of movies, books and music as well as to many kinds of lifestyle choices and personalities and relationships. This is a great thing to be admired.

The comfort of Christianity is also one of personal morality. I would hate to see a world without Christianity. There would be no moral basis, only greedy enjoyment, I presume. The Christian God offers so much solace also from the fact that people behave better and people want to be better human beings. Christianity is the only religion which emphasizes moral wisdom. No secular book guarantees moral wisdom and personal morality like the Bible wants to do.

I don't want to live in a moral jungle or live a moral puberty without a sophisticated, wise book that guarantees elevation, dignity and celebration of the most vulnerable citizens. No bar, no night club, no nocturnal, drunken hearsay comes with their beastliness and toughness even close to the grandeur and magnificence of a Christian God which admires innocence and loves the simplistic innocence in human beings.

Fortunately, America is a Judeo-Christian country. The most morally interesting and the most morally deep faith is being spread on United States of America which is a great relief.

The Greatest American Films of Our Century

I have always liked movies that either a) have a miraculous atmosphere that stays on my mind or b) are exceptionally touching and memorable experiences.

It is relatively difficult to find a memorable film. This film might even be a comedy that has a cheap and shallow reputation. To me Rush Hour, Dumb & Dumber, The Cable Guy and Old School are much more touching and memorable works than many artistic films respected by the critics such as Piano Teacher and Manderlay.

Concerning films, I usually tend not to like minimalism. European films make me vomit from time to time. Bad mood, depression and nihilism are not profound things. The battle between good and evil and the moments that touch the soul are more profound. Greatness, dignity, et cetera. However, The Lives of Others and Baader Meinhof Complex are refreshing exceptions, like for example the films of Kieslowski.

I mostly like films that are Films with a big F. An epic take and a pervasive, all-inclusive description of a single subject appeals to me more. A film has to have a Maker behind it.

I am more interested in what happens in two or three hours than the plot. I don't like too ordinary films, films that have just something and I search for the most mind-blowing experience, a great film which is like music.

Overrated films are (in my opinion) the talkies of Greta Garbo, the comedies of the Marx Brothers and Mel Brooks, the filmography of Kurosawa. Yet, I hope someday to understand Kurosawa as much as I understand Bergman.

Now I want to write a list about the greatest American films of the 21st century. It is a time which almost started with the collapse of the World Trade Center buildings and continued to the Iraq war, Breivik, Brexit and the corona virus. The presidents of America have been Bush, Obama, Trump and Biden. We have lived twenty-one years of the new millennium and the new century. The entertainers and the artists that have died have been such names as Heath Ledger, Philip Seymour Hoffman, Anthony Bourdain, Chester Bennington, Amy Winehouse and Robin Williams. Concerning politics, Anna Politkovskaya, Pim Fortuyn, Anna Lindh, Benazir Bhutto and Jamal Khashoggi have all died tragically. The Finnish currency mark changed into euro in

2002. There has been five World Cups of Soccer and also five Olympic hockey tournaments.

Here is a list of the most significant American films of the 21st century (thus far)

Mulholland Drive (2001)
The most central of the films of David Lynch. A classic on the level of Vertigo and Sunset Boulevard which appear only rarely in ten years. A dream-like dive into a horrific beauty and a nightmare. This is a very central Hollywood films filled with amazing meanings that charm the mind forever.

Sideways (2004)
A film which is sold as a comedy but a film that is more like a masterful drama and an entertaining holiday film. After the film, the viewer misses the vineyards and the landscape of the summer of California. A clean, neat, tight work of art.

Brokeback Mountain (2005)
One of the most essential love stories ever. There is something essential about the love that feels so wonderful but is so rarely experienced because of the great evil of homophobia, or gay hatred (a term I like more). Ledger is amazing as Ennis Del Mar and the landscape is magnificent. An American love story.

Into the Wild (2007)
Maybe the greatest nature film ever. The entertaining escapism of a young idealist to the nature of America leaving all cities and their materialistic comfort zone. A film that is very American, to the core.

The Dark Knight (2008)
A rough, moral masterpiece. The most definitive Batman film. Ledger is the most amazing villain and I don't think anyone disagrees.

Avatar (2009)
The first great film with a virtual meta world, in addition to the real world. And the world is so fantastic, great and imaginative that it makes the film exceptionally original.

Django Unchained (2012)
A rough, moral masterpiece. The most important film of Tarantino. DiCaprio and Waltz are amazing as the extreme evil and the extreme good.

Wolf of Wall Street (2013)
A movie that has everything. An epic film with little tricks and hooks that only the experienced Martin Scorsese knows. A multi-millionaire swine and a professional

asshole Jordan Belfort hobbling the whole world to himself. The most charismatic role of DiCaprio since Titanic. A sort of a guy movie with its raw, naughty humour.

Birdman (2014)
A masterpiece of small area. A theatre which is depicted in a narrow, addictive way. Claustrophilia. A zone that stays in the mind. The dialogue is magnificent.

The Shape of Water (2017)
A sugary, sympathetic and a kind film. Choreographically brilliant. A film that makes you want to drown in its green rain even though the brutal villain is depressingly cruel.

My Relationship with Classic American Television

As I have mentioned, I love the classics in everything. The thought of American television shows always fill me with great sense of awe and wonder. I usually think about the places in which they are situated in. I see great valleys of American decades wherein the shows descend onto American living-rooms where millions of families enjoy the greatest television shows of each decade. It is a fascinating, phenomenal world in which to settle in. I also enjoy the brainlessness of the feeling. I think brainless wonder and unconscious speculation makes the viewing experience great and with some company the shows would be even greater to enjoy. I recently watched the first two episodes of Band of Brothers with my friend and borrowed the DVD box set to him. It was a great experience to share the beginning of the series with him. Each decade of entertainment is precious and different from each other.

Here is a list of the television shows I want to purchase and own someday.

Partridge Family
Sanford & Son
The Beverly Hillbillies
Roseanne
Cheers
Frasier
Happy Days
Roots
Little House on the Prairie
E. R.
I Love Lucy
Love Boat
Charlie's Angels
Doctor Kildare
M.A.S.H.
Fantasy Island
Kung Fu
Golden Girls
The Facts of Life
Dynasty
The Bill Cosby Show
The A Team
Starsky & Hutch
NYPD Blue

Magnum P. I.
The Jackie Gleason Show
The Dukes of Hazzard
Three's Company
The Jeffersons
All in the Family
Mork & Mindy
Laverne and Shirley
The Six Million Dollar Man
The Bionic Woman
Maude
Rhoda
The Waltons
The Sonny and Cher Comedy Hour
Hawaii Five-O
Meltose Place
Beverly Hills 90210
The Mary Tyler Moore Show
Bonanza
Green Acres
Bewitched
Gomer Pyle, USMC
The Dick Van Dyke Show
The Jetsons
The Thunderbirds
Ren & Stimpy
Pinky and the Brain
Gunsmoke
Rawhide
The Flintstones
The Danny Thomas Show
Murphy Brown
Home Improvement
SNL
Hill Street Blues
Columbo

These don't even contain the great Friends, Seinfeld and Twin Peaks, which I already own. I also have the first season of X Files which is a masterful take on the secrets of American government and the paranormal issues which are so dear to me. Twin Peaks is a sort of mystical, secretive take on American subculture.

The Greatest American Films of the 20th Century

No one can deny how amazing the 20th century of cinema was. Fresh, innovative and continuously exciting and revolutionary. I think the 20th century showed the world the most evil and the most good that mankind has had to offer us. Everything changed in cinema and television and entertainment, and as well in literature, poetry, theatre and music. I don't want to think of Hitler, Stalin, Franco, Mao Tse-Tung or Mussolini. There was so much horrendous evil that is inexplicable and it is incredibly sad that so much good was met with so much pointless evil.

Here are my takes on the greatest American films of the 20th century.

Citizen Kane

Perhaps the greatest film ever made. The shadows of the scenes are memorable, as well as the whole point of the film, the childhood that stayed in the millionaire tycoon's mind as the most memorable time of his life even after all that fame and fortune.

Casablanca

The most beautiful love story ever. The way the tough, quiet, non-partisan, cynical and neutral Rick is revealed from the great flashback scene to be a romantic, sensitive and longing man, is absolutely brilliant. Also, the last scene is amazing and the whole film is delicately written with all the sympathetic characters. Also, this film has a dignity that few other films have.

Sunset Boulevard

Another mysterious film. The beginning is one of the greatest beginnings in history. The mansion of a former silent film star Norma Desmond is a memorable place. The greatness of the film is the loneliness and the self-deception occurring in the mansion forgetting the "boring, normal" present time in which Norma is no longer a star.

Vertigo

One of the most beautiful love stories ever. The feeling of emptiness, an empty San Francisco, is breath-taking. There are forces which control us from the top, one feels and the viewer slumbers into a nice, comforting dream where the city is tender and beautiful.

12 Angry Men

The smallest atmosphere, a room where 12 members or a jury are conversing and arguing, is just brilliant. The characters are all magnificently written and the whole room leaves a feeling that this film is much too short.

2001

The most popular philosophical film of all time, I think. The greatest science fiction has had to offer us.

One Flew Over the Cuckoo's Nest

Such a nice, memorable film that revolutionized the thought that mental health patients have rights also. The mental hospital is depicted as a big place, one that stays in the mind of the viewer for the rest of his or her life. A humane, great film and the greatest role Jack Nicholson has played.

The Shining

The vast emptiness of the Overlook Hotel is one of the most memorable places in movie history. Overlook is a place that only the few have mastered. I always want to escape to that hotel as I watch this film. The Shining is also one hell of an entertainment and a deep exploration of the unknown.

Once Upon a Time in America

The movie of my life. The way Sergio Leone depicts life itself is so incredibly touching. The bitter sweetness of youth, the warm, weary loneliness of old age, the far-away innocence of childhood, the redemption of the past in the present. The film is so epic and so profound in its exploration of the mind and the subconscious, the memory and life itself, that I consider this film in some way the greatest ever made. To me, it also feels like a mirror of my own life, my childhood, my past, my memory, my bittersweet experiences, my loneliness.

Eyes Wide Shut

The greatest night film ever. In no film the night is depicted as great as in this film. An unbelievably beautiful vision of a secret journey of one man to the secret society located in New York. A dark masterpiece which is very hard to surpass. I sometimes feel like Kubrick sent us a message of ourselves in the 21st century.

Tragic Heroes

I have always been fascinated with prematurely deceased, famous people. From the horrendous murder of John Lennon to the lonely suicide of David Strickland and the overdose of River Phoenix, heroes who died young have so often stayed in my mind as tragically lost people. I often wonder what they did few hours before passing, the innocence of their stardom compared with the brutality of their destiny. I am fascinated by the fact that no one knew that they would die soon after their fame. It often comes as a surprise that a well-known legend dies and it seems that God takes from us the most talented souls early (not always, of course). The fact that a comedian like Phil Hartman left us so much innocent and happy-go-lucky comedy is tragically contrasted with his amazingly dark and sad death from his wife who shot him to his bed and then turned the gun on herself.

There is something mystical about being interested in these people. It is because they didn't know. But also, thinking about legendary Finns that died prematurely, one is immensely interested in their fate. In Finland there have been people like Harri Sirola, Mandi Lampi, Pete Walli, Seppo Heikinheimo and Kirsti Härkönen who left an indelible mark into my soul. One of sadness and longing, for the beautiful life of theirs, so young, so talented, was cut short by a horrendously tragic decision. Those five Finns all committed suicide and their decisions shook Finland. The loss is so sad and the feeling is filled with a touching love of those fallen souls.

I am listening to John Lennon's Imagine right now as I write this. The fact that Lennon was gunned down near his house in New York City, is such a strange and painful fact, when compared with the greatness of his music. The news of a fallen celebrity always comes as a surprise, which fills the mind with curiosity. The details of the last days are more intriguing than the mind of a psychopath. I sometimes feel guilt over being so interested in the dead celebrities but I tend to hate the stories of psychopathic serial killers because it feels like social pornography and a bit immoral like the killer is elevated and treated like an interesting person. I don't want to be interested in the lives that some serial killer ended or in the mind of a monster.

Kurt Cobain, Layne Staley, Marilyn Monroe, John F. Kennedy, Robert F. Kennedy, John F. Kennedy Jr., Sharon Tate, Martin Luther King, Malcolm X. Life is filled with unlucky men and women. It seems that in 20th century, a premature death was almost like a rule, than an exception. I tried to commit suicide in 2014, when I started to hear voices, but I failed. Now, almost six years later, I am endlessly happy that I failed. It would have been the saddest thing I know, to my parents and to my brothers. I also have a lot of work to do here, concerning my art. It is not my time to leave this planet yet.

America has its own dead tragic heroes, more than any other country, I think. It is not the most glorious fact about the country but it is still psychologically a very interesting thing, one has to admit, even after all the suffering and the tragedy.

Americans and the Rest of the World

I have often wondered how Americans see the rest of the world. The reputation of Americans is that they are embarrassingly ignorant about the rest of the world but this is not completely true at all.

Do they become enthralled over Ingmar Bergman and ABBA and at that time really desire to feel Swedish? I know some who do this. And it is always a great feeling when this happens. I have even thought of them thinking about Swedish language while watching Bergman and thinking how beautiful a language it is. Or concerning ABBA, the appreciation of the great music but also the fact that ABBA knows English so well.

I have sometimes also thought what they think of Finnish language and Finnish music on YouTube. Finlandia by Jean Sibelius, for example. I feel like me knowing Finnish like my back pockets is a great, secretive skill that many Americans don't have.

I know many Finnish-Americans, through Facebook, who live in America while being proud of their Finnish heritage. It is always a supreme feeling to be a real Finn in that group because I feel like I have knowledge of the Finnish culture, language and way of life, which they don't necessarily have.

I guess my view of Americans is that they are strong and respectable and masculine and simple people. I often play a scenario in my mind of an aggressively thinking, non-nuanced American whose love for the rest of the world is in its curiosity very touching and surprising. I like the surprise, the feeling of touching surprise that he might suddenly be in love with our culture.

How I wish to explain them Americans our Finland's Finnish feelings. The photographs where my loved ones celebrate, the beautiful nature we could walk together, the great world-class music like Chisu and Jenni Vartiainen, PMMP and CMX, the ice hockey games from the 1995-1999 when a team Tappara played, from my hometown Tampere, our infamous artists like Kalervo Palsa, Timo K. Mukka and Harri Sirola, for example.

Then I think about the letters ö and ä and different kinds of dialects we Finns have and the complexity of our words and names. I feel that there is the simple names like Hervanta, Helsinki, Nokia, Espoo, Pori, Rovaniemi and Vaasa. And then we have the very difficult names and words like Äystö, Puljujärvi, rypäle and öykkäri.

The modern Finland has also a cornucopia of great-sounding, aesthetic first names which reveal that Finland has grown into something else, something more civilized and more stylish, so to speak. We used to have names like Jorma, Martti ja Pertti which are thought of as hillbilly names and not cool, modern names. Nowadays we have boy's names like Sebastian, Patrik, Aron, Miro, Joakim, Eeli and Kristian. Also, the names for Finnish baby girls in the modern Finland, tend to be more modern, rich and beautiful with names like Janette, Sofia, Fanniina, Olivia, Riikka-Mari and Sini-Petra. Nowadays, names like Kyllikki, Orvokki or Sinikka are more like names for octogenarians.

Why Donald Trump Felt Like a Revenge of Lonely People?

Whenever I watch the election battle between Hillary Clinton and Donald Trump from 2016, I am struck by a curious feeling which satisfies me deeply and which feels good. Clinton was the absolute favourite of media, the celebrities, the experts, the popular, the sexy and the good. Everyone thought that she would win 100-0. Everyone was certain of it. Dozens and dozens of people like George Clooney and Nancy Pelosi repeated one another in the firm official truth – Donald Trump will never become the president. The victory of Clinton and the defeat of Trump had remained so certain in people's minds that its powerful hyping now seems like an idiotic hysteria.

I have also thought of a clip on Real Time with Bill Maher where a conservative commentator Ann Coulter is asked who is the most likely Republican candidate to win the candidacy for president of the United States. Coulter answered "of the declared ones Donald Trump." After saying this, Coulter received a rambunctious laughter from the whole studio audience as well as the panel.

Afterwards, I have thought of the election thoroughly. Hillary, a woman, who was marketed as a sensible, stabile, sane, wise and strong woman who is the decision of all good people versus Donald Trump, the goofy, ridiculous male candidate thought to be by many as an insane bigot and a dangerous narcissist. The same Trump who had said on a bus in 2005 to a reporter called Billy Bush that he likes to "grab women by the pussy." Nonsense-speaking, angry, miserable and hate-filled Trump competed against Clinton, the decent an strong heroine of the female sex. The situation seemed like a masterful battle which is difficult to imagine or to create.

When Donald Trump won, against the steady and cocksure certainty of the world that he would lose, many young and hopeful Clinton supporters were crying because a woman would not be the president and the awful male candidate had won. The strident and aggressive Trump had won and he took the victory laconically and humbly. Many people were left speechless.

One reason for the loss of Clinton was probably her inauthentic behaviour. Her campaign was boosted by performers like Beyonce and Jay-Z who were most likely not her favourite musicians and were part of the campaign just because they were popular and perfect as well as being on her side. She wasn't as casual as Trump, who was thought to be more authentic even though Trump was more aggressive. Also, the term "stronger together" sounded platitudinous and lame compared to the interesting and ingenious "make America great again". America is quite an individualistic country.

For some reason I felt that the election was a revenge from those who work and work without getting a thank you from it and a revenge from the fact that many people get glory from mere existing and posing and messing around. They are these "young, media sexy, lusted and desired" people whose every comment, post, thought, feeling and decision is wonderful, lovely, perfect and natural by hundreds or hundreds of thousands of people. I am of course referring to Instagram culture and the empty shallowness and celebrity of it.

The victory of Trump felt like the lonely ones and the lonely workers, the makers of sensible things, finally got one of the most satisfying and sweet revenge from the popular and the sexy, from the perfect and the desired, those who are always supported by a large groups, compared to the people who have no group.

They who are always liked. Against those who are not spoken of and who cause an awkward silence. They whose thoughts and feelings are not as important as the rest of us. They who seem pathetic and lonely. They who don't have any position in the social game.

Why Family Matters – A Conservative Mindset

My own notion of my own family is that we are more cautious than others. We often see the outer world as wrong and the family right. As a family I mean my mother, my deceased father and my two brothers. Often, the so-called experts want you to search yourself and to liberate yourself through the battles and challenges of life. The experts are particularly loathsome when they attack my upbringing and my personality and want to become my parents. I don't want to search myself and liberate myself just because someone says so and I feel that I have found myself and liberated myself by achieving and thinking and feeling. I do not like unimportant risks and constant openness to new kinds of ways of thinking through human experiences because I can do it myself as well. I find myself divine and godly so I don't have to find bad thoughts and bad ways of living because they don't work in my case. I am my own teacher. Still, I don't deny the importance of other people, but they have to be my friends and supporters, or my future soul mate, so I can affirm the importance of them.

Also, my own family has taught me that the outdoors really are dangerous and obnoxious, at times. I feel like as a conservative person the disgusting or disappointing things come from the outside – from people who don't understand me or like me. It is always those young or old left-wingers who think the world is such a nice and wonderful place because they don't have to suffer in it. Therefore, they don't think that any harm can happen to them or the Western world, for example.

It still feels quite bitter the way in which the outer world has wounded me. I really don't like wounds and I like being invisible. Invisibility means that I don't like to be open on Facebook and be center of the attention anywhere. I find privacy, the fact that I have privacy, to be an exquisitely secret feeling. It feels like warm water flowing through my body all the time. Most Facebook posts are the cause of obsession and addiction.

What feels right, is right. What feels wrong, is wrong. We are told to be open and liberated. But we are told it by a great lie. We never examine what that openness and liberation is. I feel like most openness has caused me harm. Whenever I take part in a conversation, an argument or try a new thing, it has caused me bitter and wrong feelings and the experience has been cruel and wrong and pointless.

Whatever they said, my own experience was more right. I think that that sentence is the story of my life. Many people can believe in a lie and only one person can believe in truth. I see it happening in many things. Life outside with the wrong people is tragic. Life outside with the right people, is not tragic and is the way in which I want to live my life.

My American Friends

I have had fun with going to internet and listen to some of my favourite people in the world. For three decades I have listened to the most interesting people I know. I call these people my American friends. Here are some of them and why I like them.

Dennis Prager

I don't know where I would be without Dennis Prager, philosophically and morally. He is the greatest moralist I know. He talks about issues in a way that is irreplaceable. Emphasizing morality, good behaviour, kindness and happiness, he is to morality what Bach is to music. When one considers the fact that most people hate even to mention morality in their lives, comparing it to the spooky moralism, Prager seems refreshingly conservative on this issue. So few people think about good and evil, morality and right and wrong, like Prager does. Most people tend to think about tolerance and intolerance more than good and evil or right and wrong. He also talks about the greatness of capitalism in a refreshingly singular way. Most people hate capitalism while enjoying all of its pleasurable goods and the liberty that enabled them to succeed.

Michael Knowles

I have thought of Michael Knowles being like an older brother to me. He has that kind of nice aura. I like his oratory and I agree with him on issues like the evil of abortion and the sin of limitless sexuality. I have found that sexuality, when it is without limits, is a sin because it overlooks the spiritual greatness of man and helps people commit to an emotionally cold way of life, soullessness to be exact. I for one consider myself a man who has one woman only, the woman I want to meet in the future and fall in love with her. I have tried prostitutes in my past and I have had almost ten very disappointing dates, and I can assure you that my experiences were very boring and pointless. The only important thing about sexuality in my life is when I meet a soul mate and want to make love with her. Other than that, it is all boring. Also, sex is something that is not comparable to hand-washing or brushing one's teeth. It is more noble, more sacred, more great than that.

Knowles also talks about issues like a wise, young master of morality. I find it sad that not that many people in Europe listen to him. His analyses on woke issues are priceless.

Michael Moore

I love Michael Moore. I find him a great moralist and a kind man with a great heart. I certainly don't buy into the usual conservative notion of him hating America. I find that he has been demonized with a blind hate from his opponents. Concerning America, it is okay to talk about its flaws. Moore has exposed the Flint water crisis and has spoken a lot about the pollution of rivers caused by giant oil companies.

I always love to hear Michael speak. He is one of those rare celebrities who have a memorable personality and a beautiful mind. When I think about people being either conservative or leftist, I think to myself that both of these factions have their own narrative, which always doesn't talk about everything, for example, the conservative narrative is blind to certain immoralities and gross grievances and the leftist narrative is also blind sometimes.

Michael Moore is a guy I would like to have a beer with. He is very authentic and real also. I have enjoyed his films. I loved when he did a bit about Finland's education for his 2015 documentary film Where to Invade Next. It made be proud to be a Finn. In it, he speaks with the moral giants of Finnish education, grown Finnish men and women who build this society of ours. They are the teachers of our schools where Finnish students succeed by doing less. I have noticed that Finland has a huge amount of people instilling goodness in our society, goodness that has become like a tradition that needs to be continued and cherished. Moore hinted at the American education as being dumb because it concentrates too much on standardized testing and homework and long hours of studying. The Finnish model, helps the students to learn what makes the happy. It is very compassionate to the students, unlike America's model, presumably.

Joe Rogan

I think The Joe Rogan Experience is the greatest podcast of our time.

The way he talks to people, from all political sides, is very authentic and touching.

I like his masculinity, his compassion for different kinds of people, his open-mindedness to all kinds of stories and his lust for life, loving in a masculine, deep way all everything about pop culture and culture in general.

It is hard to put him in a box. I find these kinds of people are also important. If everyone was partisan, with predictable, clustering opinions, we would have nothing but culture wars without any sense of tolerance or lovingness for people.

I love when he talks about the JFK conspiracy, the insane genius of Stanley Kubrick and all kinds of talented artists and comics as well as the gossip revolving people's current situations. I also love when he talks about the vices – like whiskey, cigarettes, fast food, pot and psychedelic drugs.

He is like a king, the guy who everyone comes to talk to, a guy who everyone admires and a guy who is the great communicator, of the greatest conversations.

Cornel West

Cornel West is one of the most precious and most important people on the planet. The reason he is so important is his unique lovingness and endless passion. There is something deeply universal about him, like he has lived a thousand years, and he loves everybody as deeply as those thousand years. It is very rare to hear a man speak about the issues with so much love as he does. He finds goodness in every one and brings the best out of every one. His love is deep and wide and passionate. One of the greatest moments was him talking to Joe Rogan for two hours and opening about music, the arts and politics so warm-heartedly. He calls all people brothers and sisters, white people as "vanillas" and black people as "chocolates." I love that, because it is said in such a loving way.

Sometimes I think that West is lonely in his gentleness. I think I am a gentle moralist, but West is greater in his gentleness, because even I think I am very far away from the greatness of his gentleness, the way he cares for everyone with such a big heart and loves everyone.

Ben Shapiro

A computer brain like me. (A computer brain is a Finnish expression, tietokoneaivo in Finnish)

When Ben Shapiro wrote an article about the ten greatest directors of our time, he declared William Wyler as the greatest director ever. I found this curious and I started to buy the films of William Wyler because I was so interested in Shapiro's personality. I found The Letter and The Best Years of Our Lives great but The Westerner and The Collector were boring for me. I have pondered about his decision and I find it weird that he praises Wyler because some of Wyler's films are still somewhat bad in my opinion. But my stance can change as time goes by.

However, Shapiro is a solid cultural commentator. He usually tells about phenomena that pisses him off and sometimes I am pissed off as well. I think he judges people too much and too easily but I find him very sharp and incisive. I also admire his sexual piety and sexual morality but I don't always agree with him on everything. I always like what he has to say on things.

Bill Maher

I decided to type the first things I know about Bill Maher. I typed the words – funny, easy-going, important and legend. I also typed "funnier than Bob Hope, Bill Cosby, Johnny Carson, Rodney Dangerfield and Don Rickles combined. The third thing I typed was "some of the greatest jokes of our lifetime."

The cool and subtle Maher is a kind of a modern institution. His program Real Time with Bill Maher is one of the greatest things of the 21st century. His former program Politically Incorrect is like a nostalgic, wistful return to the 1990s when Americans seemed more unified and the celebrities seemed more authentic and talented.

His stand-up specials are all amazing and unique. Whereas most comedians tell boring jokes about small, boring subjects, Maher tells jokes about important issues such as feminism, health care and religion. I loved Be More Cynical, Victory Begins at Home and I'm Swiss. They are the three greatest specials from this hyper-talented, super-smart comedian.

On Becoming Faithful

So, I feel American. How have I gone from Finland to this feeling?

American values and American culture fill up some kind of void. I believe that this is
not a spiritual void, this is more like a void that is spiritual, but doesn't find its match,
in its greatness. The options in one's own country, be it Finland, Sweden or Poland or
Germany, are not enough in a modern, technological, pluralistic world and one has to
find heroes and ideals in something more grandiose than one's own country. Finland
is only the size of Kentucky in a world that is much more bigger than Finland. The
charming and tempting options for a spiritual and moral hunger stem sometimes from
conservative, Judeo-Christian values. It is like a canvas on which one can imagine
oneself as something larger than life. One's own country isn't always enough. Even
Americans can feel this way about their own country.

How have I become so faithful to America?

There is something deep about the connection I have towards America but I have
never analysed what it is. Now I think it is the combination of inspiration and
gratitude. It is exciting and charismatic to feel American while living in Finland. It is
also a vengeful feeling to my Finnish wounds from the past. Mostly, it is a secret
bond to the country that always consoled me in my worst moments. A grateful feeling
of an extremely satisfying friendship, with the most consoling and exciting friend in
the world.

Some Finns are admirers of certain American things. When I was in army our captain
had a book shelf filled with literature about Reagan and America. I don't know what
he felt about America and how much he loved Finland and America. One politician
of ours has also said that Finland needs American ethos more. I agree. Some Finns
were supporters of Donald Trump. But I never know if my Finn contemporaries are
ashamed of their love for America, sometimes over Finland. It is like they are Finns
but like Trump, as a way of giving the finger to the left-wing hegemony in Finland,
but at the same time, one does not know how they love America. How faithful are
they?

Sometimes it is time to step out of the closet as a lover of America and many aspects
of conservatism. To become faithful. But faithfulness in the closet is okay as well, a
faithfulness which is the result of much thinking and admiring, finding one's own
voice, without the need to talk about them that much out in the open.

Why I Am Anti-Anti-American

I first learned about the stupidity of anti-Americanism from a community I was in. This socialist community preferred everyone to have the same opinions as everyone else. The community taught that consumerism is somehow bad, even though it is everyone's own choice to consume or not. Once they held a meeting in outdoors, in downtown Tampere to protest climate change. I for one don't believe in global warming destroying the whole world, as I have read data that climate change is completely natural. So if I would go to the meeting to protest climate change, I would lie to myself, because I really don't believe in it.

Also, the hatred towards capitalism, conservatism and religiosity was self-evident in the community. A secular, socialist community it was, a very predictable in its opinions.

One woman even said that North Korea and the United States of America are equally bad societies. I replied that "there is a little difference still. In America there is no totalitarianism." Then the woman replied that Guantanamo Bay is torture and thus America is equally bad as North Korea.

Once the same woman said that the conservative Finns party are a bunch of physically repulsive men. She offended their looks and referred to a meme where the men's faces were.

I imagine, is this the moral compass of Finns? The greatest symbol of freedom and innovation is laughed at and countries like North Korea are viewed morally equivalent of the absolute best country in the world? Everyone has to have the same opinions? Everyone has to think alike in every situation?

Anti-Americanism is dreadful because it doesn't know how great things actually are. It doesn't respect freedom, it laughs at it, while at the same time enjoying it. It doesn't know anything about the nature of evil, how different evil states are compared to free states. It doesn't care about fighting evil, as the evil of multiculturalism shows us.

Concerning these issues I am a proud anti-anti-American. I still think pacifism and peace are respectable endeavours and I completely understand people who are anti-war. But anti-Americanism perverts goodness and evil in a way that is dangerous and foolish. America is not China. America is not Russia. China and Russia as the world's policemen is a horrendous notion. Without America we would drown.

My Left-Wing Sympathies

I can't deny that left-wingers are more empathetic in their approach to human affairs. They are more inclined to listen, to understand different points of view and to expand their imagination into all kinds of ways to live. Left-wingers also talk about societal ills which the conservatives usually don't want to talk about because conservatives are sometimes blind to the ills of their own society.

Also, I really cannot deny that people of the left have traditionally been much more talented than people of the right. I can name countless actors, actresses, musicians, authors, poets and film-makers who have tended towards left. The same list for conservatives consist only a handful names. This is probably due to the fact that left-wingers are more open-minded to think things in many ways than rigid conservatives are.

I think that on the issues like police brutality, education, health care the left-wingers are a force to be reckoned with. I think that left-wingers are also intellectually more mature than right-wingers. When I want to listen to a person who appreciates the fact that I don't work at this moment, I choose the leftist. Right-wingers are all about work, work, work as if participating in the treadmill every single day is a sign of liberty. Left-wingers also tend to appreciate artists and artistic freedom more than right-wingers.

The Young Turks is a great example of left-wing reasonableness. The hosts Cenk Uygur and Ana Kasparian are incredibly intelligent and empathetic towards the weakest of American society. I am impressed by them. They are angelic voices of reason when the right-wing of America goes too far in some cases.

Even though woke culture, a product of the left, has been a dominant cultural force, unfortunately, the collective denunciation of racism, homophobia, transphobia and sexism is not at all a bad way to build a great, humane and functioning society. Deeming those evil things as evil by making them socially unacceptable doesn't sound bad at all in my opinion.

The Paradise of the West

I spend my days, mostly, on the internet. Every third day I go to visit my mother, who is a widow, and I take out the trash, go to the food market and sometimes make food with her. I also go to a library to borrow different kinds of books to her, I go to the library approximately twice a month.

Next year 2022, I will apply for university of applied sciences to study film-making. I want to be a film-maker in the future. Now I am enjoying the final moments of not working, only writing before I can finally, possibly, hopefully enjoy the community of other future film-makers, in 2022.

I have a simple life, a lonesome life or actually a quiet, peaceful life without many friends, but a few close one. I don't flash my personality on the Instagram nor do I post on Facebook every day.

I smoke twenty cigarettes a day and drink a lot of Coca Cola or other sodas in a day (drinking sodas is a great addition that helps my writing.)

I am incredibly blessed by capitalism, or as some Finns would like to call it, a market economy. I can order food, drinks, clothing, films, books from countless stores on the internet. I can walk to a nearby supermarket and buy anything I need. I can participate in the re-shaping of the supermarket, as in what items I would like to buy there, items that are not at the moment being sold there. I can go to the city via bus, tramway or a taxi. The people who provide services to me are all very nice and want the best for me.

I am also endlessly grateful for the fact that my life is financed by the state because I have had a very tragic and difficult upbringing. I am a firm believer in the welfare state, a state where most people actually grow society and put the welfare of its citizens paramount. When I say that my life is financed by the state, I want to stress the fact that not everyone in Finland has to participate in the rat race, as in working themselves to death. I find it more empathetic to love everyone regardless of whether they pay taxes or not. Also, the money I receive is spent and money in a welfare state revolves. Also, concerning rat race or treadmill, if everyone worked all the time, we wouldn't have no days where we had great passions and great passions are important but they also demand leisure time a lot.

I am also grateful for the security of my hometown Tampere. This is the most alluring city to live in Finland at this moment. Tampere surpasses Helsinki in its reputation of being a great city for its citizens.

I have freedom of speech and I can spend my life expressing myself through my passions and interests.

Everything works here. Everything is simple, easy-going and fun. Everything also gets better all the time. The market economy corrects itself here. In Finland, I am not left alone. I consider this the paradise of the West. I am not one of those people who constantly badmouth the West. I am very proud of this thing called the Western civilization.

I have all the information of the world on my computer.

And I get to watch my American friends on YouTube while reading the news about people's lives on Facebook.

What more is there?